W9-CKT-527

STEVE JOBS

BY SARA GREEN

BELLWETHER MEDIA • MINNEAPOLIS, MN

Jump into the cockpit and take flight with Pilot books. Your journey will take you on high-energy adventures as you learn about all that is wild, weird, fascinating, and fun!

This edition first published in 2015 by Bellwether Media, Inc.

No part of this publication may be reproduced in whole or in part without written permission of the publisher. For information regarding permission, write to Bellwether Media, Inc., Attention: Permissions Department, 5357 Penn Avenue South, Minneapolis, MN 55419.

Library of Congress Cataloging-in-Publication Data

Green, Sara, 1964-
  Steve Jobs / by Sara Green.
    pages cm. – (Pilot. Tech Icons)
  Summary: "Engaging images accompany information about Steve Jobs. The combination of high-interest subject matter and narrative text is intended for students in grades 3 through 7"– Provided by publisher.
  Audience: Age 7-12.
  Includes bibliographical references and index.
  ISBN 978-1-60014-994-8 (hardcover : alk. paper)
  1. Jobs, Steve, 1955-2011–Juvenile literature. 2. Computer engineers–United States–Biography–Juvenile literature.
3. Businesspeople–United States–Biography–Juvenile literature. 4. Apple Computer, Inc.–History–Juvenile literature. I.
Title.
  QA76.2.J63G73 2014
  338.7'61004092–dc23
  [B]
                            2014015805

Printed in the United States of America, North Mankato, MN.

TABLE OF CONTENTS

CHAPTER 1

WHO IS STEVE JOBS?

Steve Jobs was a brilliant business and technology leader. As **co-founder** and **CEO** of Apple Inc., his ideas changed how people use computers and phones. Over time, he introduced the world to the iPhone, iPad, and other popular products. He also helped **revolutionize** how people listen to music with the iPod. As CEO of Pixar Animation Studios, he changed the way people make **animated movies**. He helped bring Sheriff Woody, Dory, and many other beloved characters to life.

Steve's success gave him fame and money. He topped the list of highest paid CEOs in the United States. However, Steve did not seek out this wealth. His curiosity and creativity inspired him to pursue different work challenges. He especially enjoyed discovering new ways to use technology. Steve demanded perfection in his products. He was passionate about their designs, both inside and out. This attention to detail paid off. Today, Steve's products are as popular as ever.

ICON BIO

Name: Steven Paul Jobs

Birthday: February 24, 1955

Died: October 5, 2011

Hometown: Los Altos, California

Marital status: Married Laurene Powell in 1991

Children: Three girls and one boy

Hobbies/ Interests: Music, reading, electronics, nutrition

CHAPTER 2

GROWING UP IN CALIFORNIA

Steve was born on February 24, 1955, to two university students. They were not married and could not take care of him. They decided to give him up for **adoption**. Paul and Clara Jobs adopted Steve when he was an infant. They promised to give him a good life and a college education. Steve grew up in Mountain View, California, with his adoptive sister, Patricia. His father repaired machines and his mother was an **accountant**.

From a young age, Steve enjoyed learning. He was especially interested in electronics. He spent many hours with his father tinkering with radios and televisions in the family's garage. His mother also taught him to read before he started elementary school. Once in school, Steve's behavior sometimes led to problems. He liked to play pranks, and he had trouble paying attention to teachers. However, the teachers knew Steve was very bright. His high test scores even allowed him to skip the fifth grade!

BIRTH FAMILY

Steve's birth parents are Abdulfattah "John" Jandali and Joanne Simpson. They had a second child, Mona, in 1957. Steve and Mona met for the first time in 1986. The siblings became great friends.

"You have to trust in something—your gut, destiny, life, karma, whatever. This approach has never let me down, and it has made all the difference in my life. "

— Steve Jobs

Steve attended Cupertino Junior High and Homestead High School in Cupertino, California. During the summer, he worked at an electronics company. When Steve was 16, a friend introduced him to Steve Wozniak, also known as "Woz." Although Woz was five years older than Steve, the two shared many interests. They both loved electronics, computers, and playing pranks on others!

Steve and Woz started their first business in 1972. Back then, people had to pay extra to make long distance calls. Steve and Woz built devices that fooled telephone companies. Their devices allowed people to make long distance calls for free. Steve and Woz made money selling them to people. However, they knew that this practice was illegal. After a short time, the two ended the business.

CHAPTER 3

FINDING A DIRECTION

In 1972, Steve graduated from high school. That fall, he enrolled at Reed College in Portland, Oregon. Reed College was expensive. Steve's parents could not afford the **tuition**. After 6 months, Steve dropped out. For the next 18 months, he slept in friends' dorm rooms and got free meals at a local temple. He collected bottles and picked apples at an orchard for money. He even snuck into classes at Reed without the professors' knowledge!

Steve was happy, but he felt aimless. In 1974, he got a job at a video game company as a game designer. After a few months, he saved enough money to go to India. He and a friend traveled around the country meeting new people and studying religion. The trip inspired Steve to set goals for himself. Seven months later, he returned to the United States determined to start a business. He knew his friend, Woz, could provide the perfect opportunity.

CHAPTER 4

APPLE COMPUTERS

Most people did not own computers in the 1970s. The government, universities, and large corporations used them. Some computers were as large as a room. Smaller computers looked like boxes that flashed lights on and off. However, while Steve was away, Woz had designed a new type of computer. It was smaller and easier to use than other computers.

In 1976, Steve and Woz decided to build these computers and sell them. They named their company Apple Computers after the apple farm where Steve worked. At first, they built computers in the Jobs family garage. Within a year, they outgrew the garage and moved to an office in Cupertino, California. Over time, Steve and Woz kept improving their computers. They added screens, color **graphics**, keyboards, and the **mouse**. People loved Apple computers. By the early 1980s, the two had sold over 700,000 of them. Steve was a millionaire!

"Your work is going to fill a large part of your life, and the only way to be truly satisfied is to do what you believe is great work. And the only way to do great work is to love what you do."

— Steve Jobs

THE FIRST APPLE

The first Apple computer was called the Apple I. Its price tag was $666.66. The company earned $774,000 from this computer.

CHAPTER 5

THE NEXT STEPS

As Apple Computers grew, more **executives** joined the company. Steve disagreed with how they wanted to run Apple. In 1985, he **resigned** from Apple Computers to start a new computer company called NeXT. It made powerful computers that used an advanced **operating system**. However, the computers were expensive and did not sell well. During this time, Steve was also leading Pixar Animation Studios, a company he bought in 1986.

By 1996, Apple Computers was losing money. Another company called Microsoft **dominated** the computer market. Apple needed new products to boost its sales. It also needed a better operating system. NeXT had just what it needed. That year, Apple bought NeXT for around $400 million. Steve returned to Apple and soon became CEO. He worked long hours to develop great new products. Within a year, Steve introduced the world to the iMac. This stylish computer was colorful and easy to use. It was a huge success. Apple was back on track!

"We started out to get a computer in the hands of everyday people, and we succeeded beyond our wildest dreams."

— Steve Jobs

For several years, Steve was the CEO of two companies, Pixar and Apple. Running two companies was exhausting, but Steve was up for the challenge. By 2000, Pixar had seen great success with movies such as *A Bug's Life* and *Toy Story 2*. Apple was also moving forward. The company began making electronics in addition to computers. In 2001, Steve introduced the world to the first iPod. Music lovers now had a new way to listen to their favorite songs. Then, in 2006, Disney bought Pixar. Steve was free to focus entirely on Apple.

By 2007, Steve realized how much his company had changed over the years. Apple Computers still made computers, but electronics were also top sellers. For this reason, Steve changed the company's name to Apple Inc. Today, people all over the world download music on iTunes and listen to it on their iPods. Millions of people own iPhones and iPads. Apple Inc. is one of the most successful companies in history!

A SIMPLE STYLE
Steve was known for wearing black turtlenecks, blue jeans, and sneakers when he gave public speeches.

CHAPTER 6

JOYS AND SOROWS

Steve enjoyed his work at Apple, but his private life was also important to him. In 1991, Steve married his wife, Laurene Powell, in Yosemite National Park in California. They had three children named Reed, Erin, and Eve. Steve also had a daughter, Lisa, from an earlier relationship. Steve and his family lived in Palo Alto, California. The family grew vegetables in their backyard. They also kept beehives for honey.

In 2003, Steve received the terrible news that he had **cancer**. Doctors performed surgery to remove the **tumors**. For several years after, Steve felt better. He lived his life as he always had and continued to work at Apple as its CEO. However, in 2008, Steve's health began to **decline**. In 2011, he decided to resign from Apple. Steve died at home on October 5, 2011, with his family by his side. That day, the world lost a creative genius. His memory lives on in the computers and electronics that changed the world.

RESUME

Education

Fall 1972: Reed College (Portland, Oregon)
1969-1972: Homestead High School (Cupertino, California)

Work Experience

1997-2011: CEO of Apple Computers (Name changed to Apple Inc., 2007)
1995-2006: CEO of Pixar
1986-2006: Chairman of Pixar
1985-1997: CEO of NeXT, Inc.
1976-1985: Co-founder, developer, marketer of Apple Computers
1974: Video game designer at Atari

Community Service/Philanthropy

- Donated $50 million to Stanford hospitals to fund the construction of a children's hospital and main building
- Donated millions of dollars to the Global Fund to Fight AIDS

LIFE TIMELINE

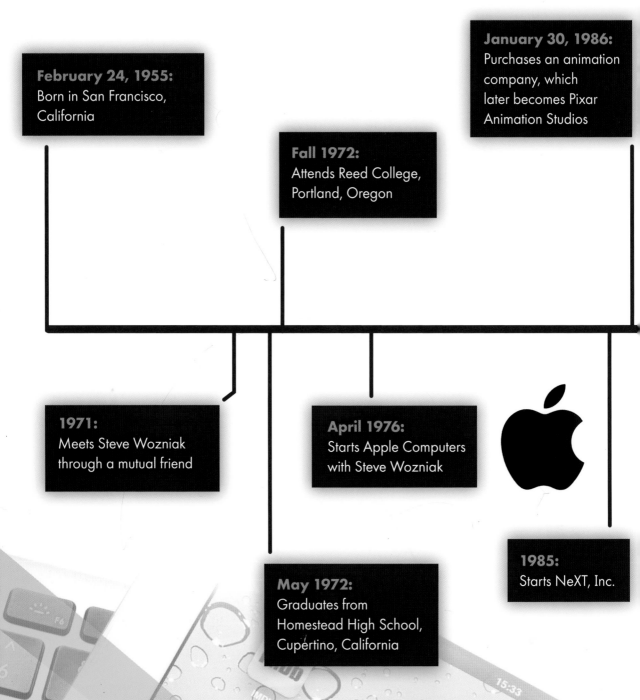

February 24, 1955:
Born in San Francisco, California

Fall 1972:
Attends Reed College, Portland, Oregon

January 30, 1986:
Purchases an animation company, which later becomes Pixar Animation Studios

1971:
Meets Steve Wozniak through a mutual friend

April 1976:
Starts Apple Computers with Steve Wozniak

May 1972:
Graduates from Homestead High School, Cupertino, California

1985:
Starts NeXT, Inc.

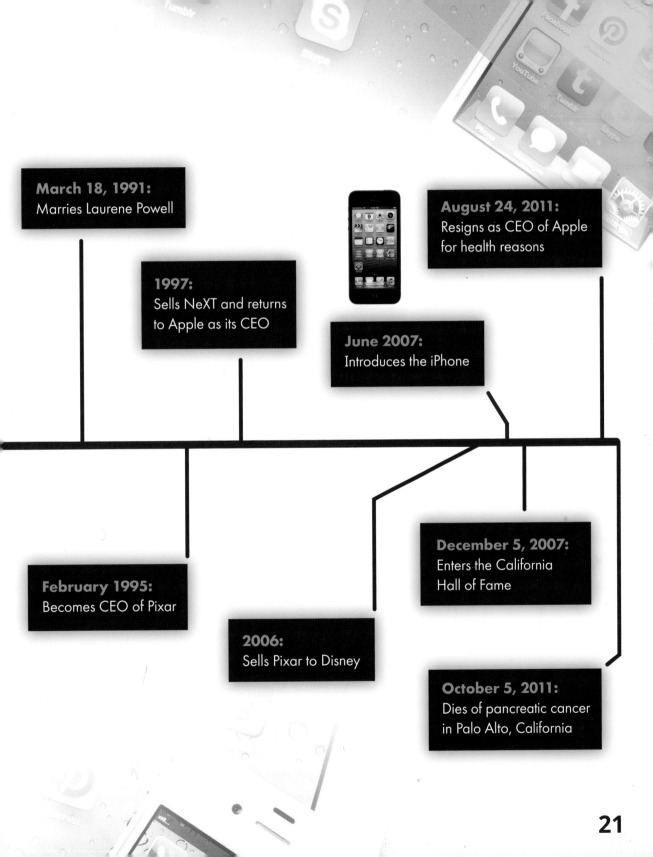

March 18, 1991:
Marries Laurene Powell

1997:
Sells NeXT and returns to Apple as its CEO

August 24, 2011:
Resigns as CEO of Apple for health reasons

June 2007:
Introduces the iPhone

February 1995:
Becomes CEO of Pixar

December 5, 2007:
Enters the California Hall of Fame

2006:
Sells Pixar to Disney

October 5, 2011:
Dies of pancreatic cancer in Palo Alto, California

GLOSSARY

accountant—a person who keeps track of the financial records of a business or person

adoption—when biological parents legally give their child to other parents to raise as their own

animated movies—movies made from a series of drawings that appear to move

cancer—a serious disease caused by cells that are not normal and that can spread to different parts of the body

CEO—Chief Executive Officer; the CEO is the highest-ranking person in a company.

co-founder—someone who starts a company with one or more people

decline—become worse

dominated—was the most powerful

executives—people in leadership positions in an organization

graphics—art such as illustrations or designs

mouse—a hand-operated device used to move a cursor around on a personal computer's screen

operating system—the main program in computers that controls the way they work; an operating system makes it possible for other computer programs to function.

resigned—left a position

revolutionize—to change something in a big way

tuition—the amount of money it costs to go to a college or university

tumors—abnormal growths of cells

TO LEARN MORE

AT THE LIBRARY

Doeden, Matt. *Steve Jobs: Technology Innovator and Apple Genius*. Minneapolis, Minn.: Lerner Publications, 2012.

Hunter, Nick. *Steve Jobs*. Chicago, Ill.: Heinemann Library, 2013.

Ziller, Amanda. *Steve Jobs: American Genius*. New York, N.Y.: HarperCollins, 2012.

ON THE WEB

Learning more about Steve Jobs is as easy as 1, 2, 3.

1. Go to www.factsurfer.com.

2. Enter "Steve Jobs" into the search box.

3. Click the "Surf" button and you will see a list of related web sites.

With factsurfer.com, finding more information is just a click away.

INDEX